monday morning®

HANDS-ON LETTERS
Pocket Pals

by Marilynn G. Barr

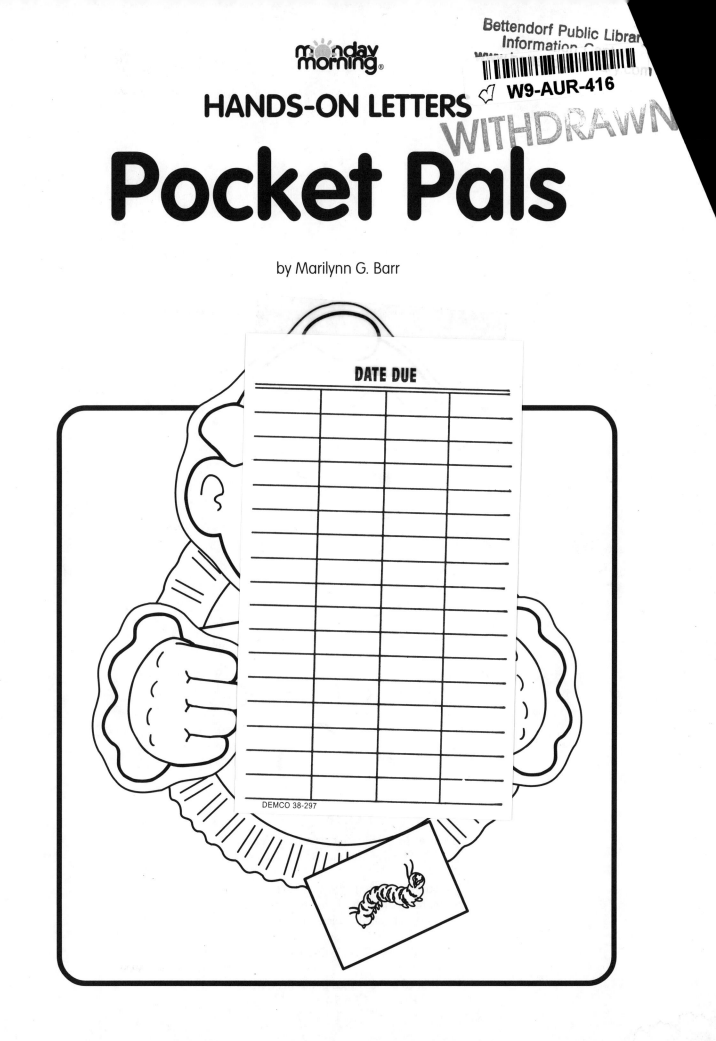

Publisher: Roberta Suid

Production: Little Acorn & Associates, Inc.

POCEKT PALS
Entire contents copyright © 2004
by Monday Morning Books, Inc.

For a complete catalog, write to the address below:
Monday Morning Books, Inc.
PO Box 1134
Inverness, CA 94937

Call our toll-free number: 1-800-255-6049
E-mail us at: MMBooks@aol.com
Visit our Web site:
http://www.mondaymorningbooks.com

ISBN 1-57612-196-8

Printed in the United States of America
9 8 7 6 5 4 3 2 1

Contents

Introduction

Pocket Pals includes alphabet pocket patterns and a variety of project ideas for creative skills practice fun. You will find a set of alphabet character pocket patterns and matching pocket picture cards for each letter of the alphabet. Each set of vowel pocket picture cards includes at least one long vowel picture. These patterns are designed for children to color, cut out, and assemble using easy-to-find supplies. A diagram of the assembled pocket pal is also included on each of the pocket pattern pages. Children will learn to recognize and match alphabet pictures and letters and develop fine motor skills. Additional Pocket Pals activities can be found on pages 62-63.

Prepare a workstation stocked with Pocket Pal patterns and a variety of craft materials for lots of creative skills practice fun. Use baskets or plastic see-through containers to organize the workstation. Store small items in separate plastic resealable bags. Use the Pocket Pals Supplies Checklist on page 6 to take inventory of supplies on-hand and needed supplies. Reproduce the Request For Craft Supplies form on page 64 for children to take home asking parents to help stock your Pocket Pals workstation.

Pocket Pals

Make 26 delightful Pocket Pals with oak tag and paper plates for children to practice identifying alphabet pictures and beginning sounds.

Materials:

Pocket Pals patterns	scissors	crayons or markers
oak tag	construction paper	paper plates
stapler	hole punch	yarn

Each child will need one and one-half paper plates. Reproduce oak tag Pocket Pals patterns for each child to color and cut out. Help each child glue the character's head at the top of the whole paper plate. Then glue the character's hands, paws, hooves, feathers, flippers, or fins to the sides of the half paper plate as shown here. Write the matching letters or reproduce, cut out, and glue a matching letter pocket (pp. 59-61) on the paper plate half. Staple the paper plates together to form a pocket. Punch a hole at the top of the Pocket Pal. Measure, cut, and tie a length of yarn through the hole. Hang finished Pocket Pals in an alphabet skills practice area when not in use. Reproduce, laminate, and cut apart the accompanying cards for each child to store in his or her pocket pal.

Poster-sized Pocket Pals

Make poster-sized Pocket Pals to display in an alphabet skills practice center.

Materials:

Pocket Pals patterns
poster board
crayons or markers
stapler
glue

oak tag
paper plates
scissors
yarn

Reproduce, color, and cut out oak tag Pocket Pals patterns (pp. 7-61). Assemble (see page 4) then glue each Pocket Pal onto a sheet of poster board. Glue the matching Pocket Pictures on the poster board around each Pocket Pal. Mount Poster-sized Pocket Pals on a wall or display board in your alphabet skills practice center.

My Alphabet Pocket Pals Portfolio

Provide children with materials to make portfolios to store and carry their Pocket Pals.

Materials:

heavy construction paper	crayons or markers	hole punch
yarn	stapler	oak tag
Pocket Pals patterns	paper plates	scissors

Provide each child with a large sheet of heavy construction paper. Have children fold construction paper to form a portfolio (diagram A). Encourage children to use crayons or markers to decorate the outside of their portfolios. Help each child punch two holes along the top of his or her portfolio (diagram B). Measure, cut, and tie a length of yarn through each set of holes to form portfolio handles.

Reproduce and help children assemble oak tag Pocket Pals (p. 4). Have children store Pocket Pals and matching Pocket Pictures inside their portfolios.

Cereal Box Pocket Pals

Make portable and easy-to-store Cereal Box Pocket Pals for individual or group alphabet skills practice.

Materials:

Pocket Pals patterns   13 cereal boxes   oak tag
construction paper   paper plates   crayons or markers
scissors   stapler   glue

Cut away the cover flaps from each of 13 large cereal boxes. Measure, cut, and glue construction paper around 13 empty cereal boxes. Reproduce, color, and cut out two sets of Pocket Pals patterns (pp. 7-61) to attach to each cereal box. Assemble (p. 4) then glue one pocket pal onto each side of a cereal box. Cut apart and place the matching sets of Pocket Pictures inside each cereal box. Children empty Pocket Pictures onto a playing surface and place only the matching cards inside the pockets. Store the cereal boxes on a shelf in your alphabet skills practice center.

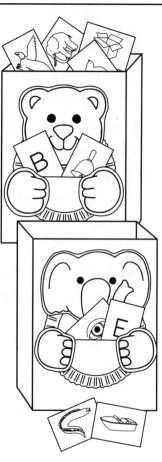

Pocket Pals Supplies Checklist

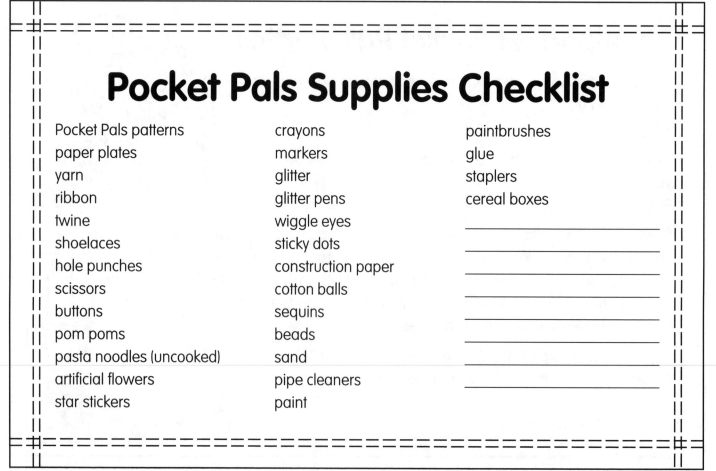

Pocket Pals patterns   crayons   paintbrushes
paper plates   markers   glue
yarn   glitter   staplers
ribbon   glitter pens   cereal boxes
twine   wiggle eyes   _____
shoelaces   sticky dots   _____
hole punches   construction paper   _____
scissors   cotton balls   _____
buttons   sequins   _____
pom poms   beads   _____
pasta noodles (uncooked)   sand   _____
artificial flowers   pipe cleaners   _____
star stickers   paint

Alligator Pocket Pal

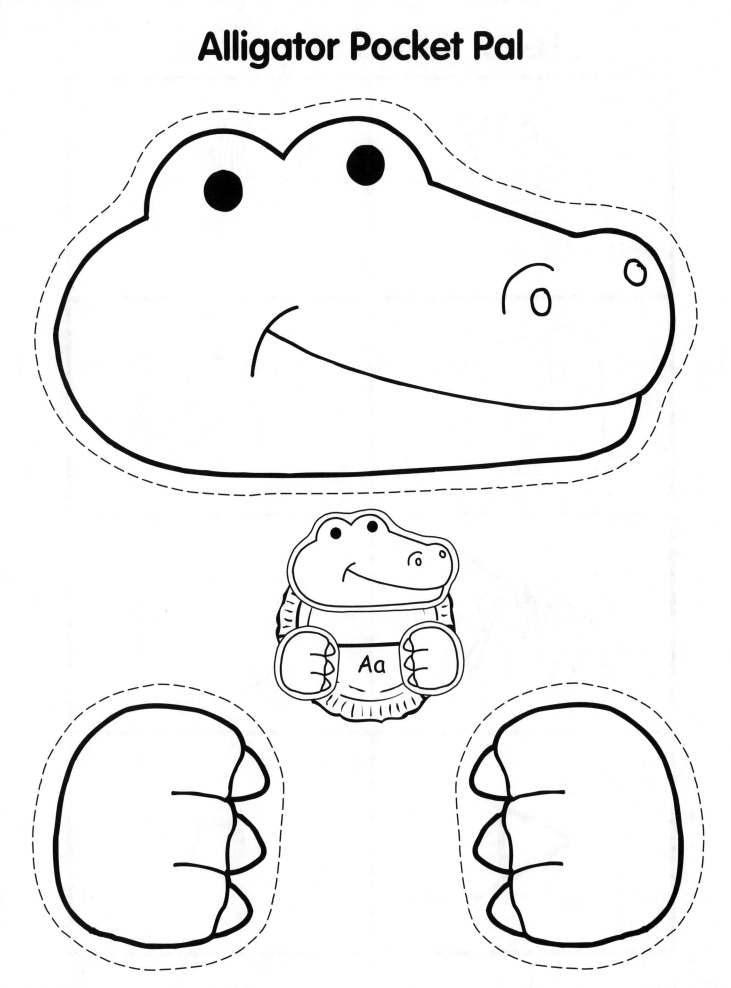

Aa

Letter A Pocket Pictures

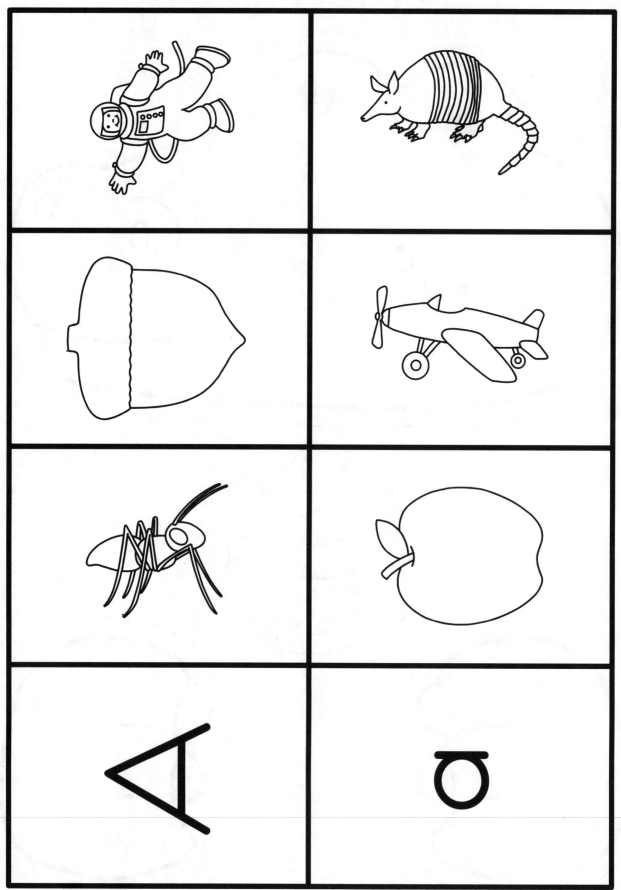

Bear Pocket Pal

Bb

Letter B Pocket Pictures

Pocket Pals • ©2004 Monday Morning Books, Inc.

Clown Pocket Pal

Letter C Pocket Pictures

Dinosaur Pocket Pal

Letter D Pocket Pictures

Elephant Pocket Pal

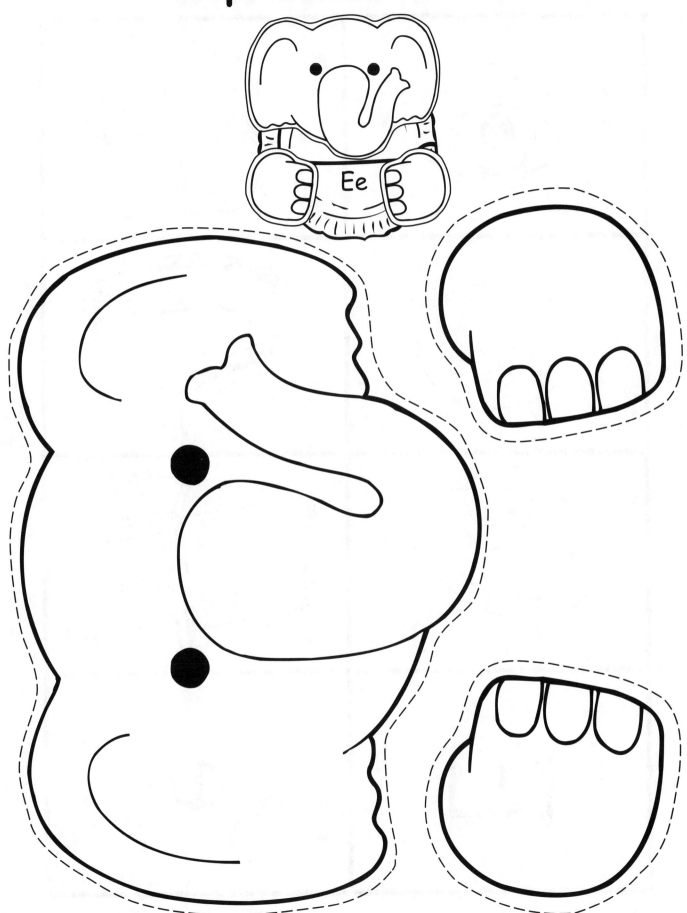

Ee

Letter E Pocket Pictures

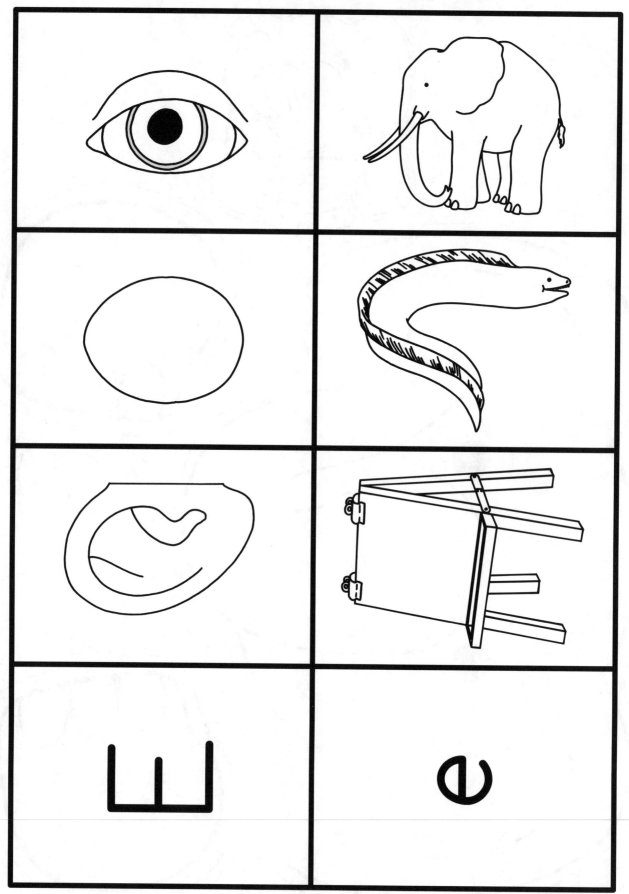

Farmer Pocket Pal

Letter F Pocket Pictures

Gorilla Pocket Pal

Letter G Pocket Pictures

Hippopotamus Pocket Pal

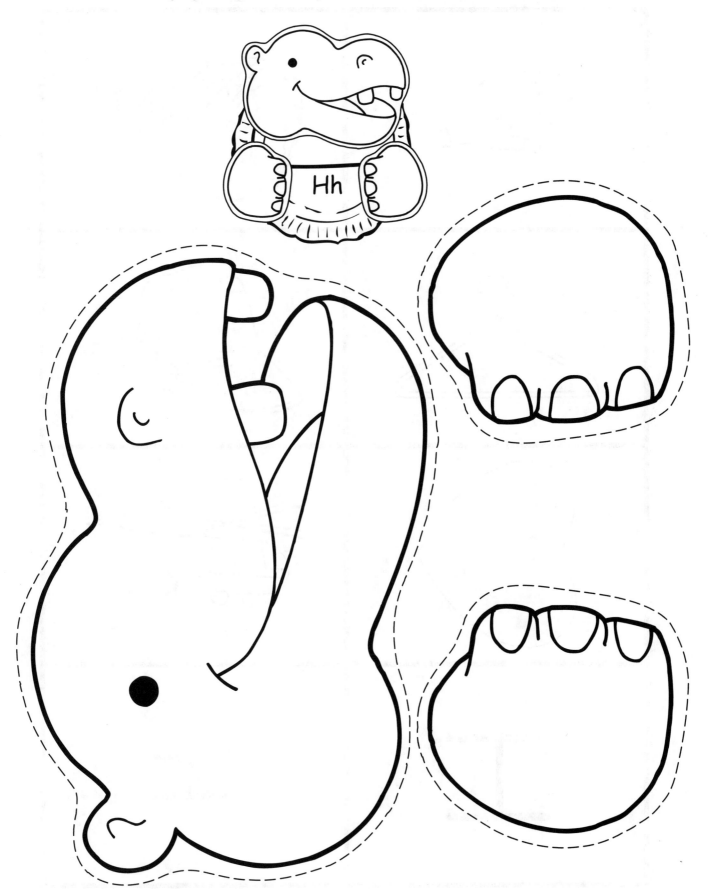

Letter H Pocket Cards

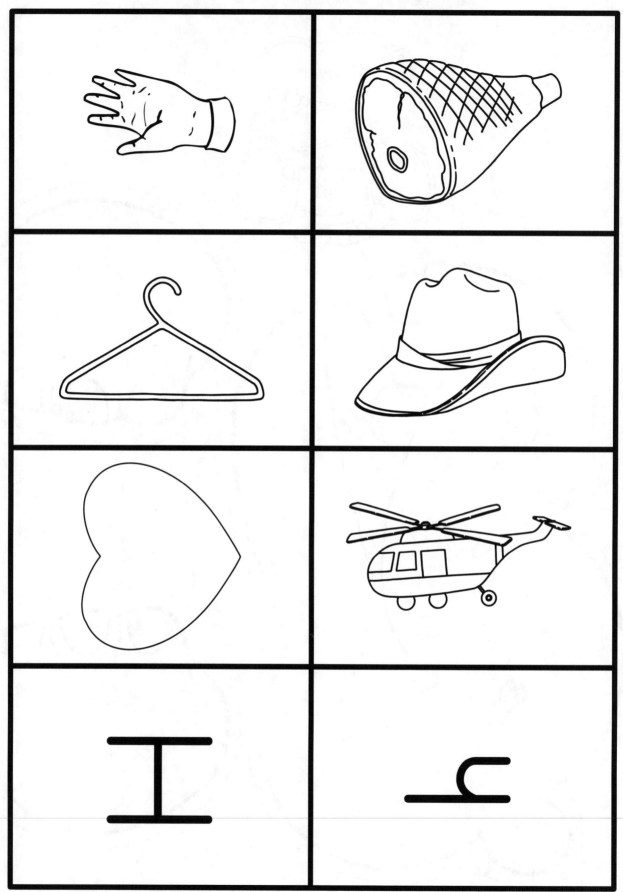

Iguana Pocket Pal

Letter I Pocket Cards

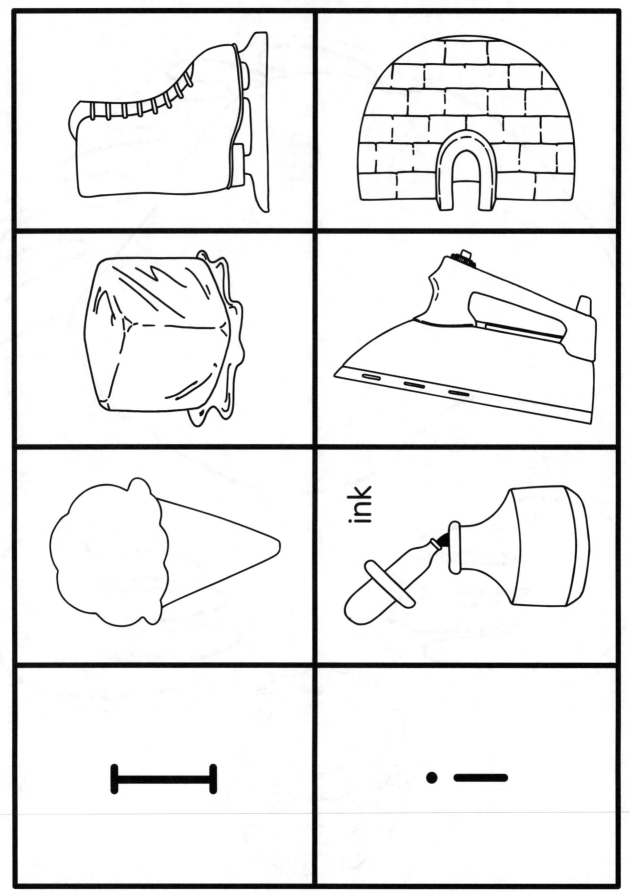

ink

Jack-in-the-box Pocket Pal

Letter J Pocket Cards

Koala Pocket Pal

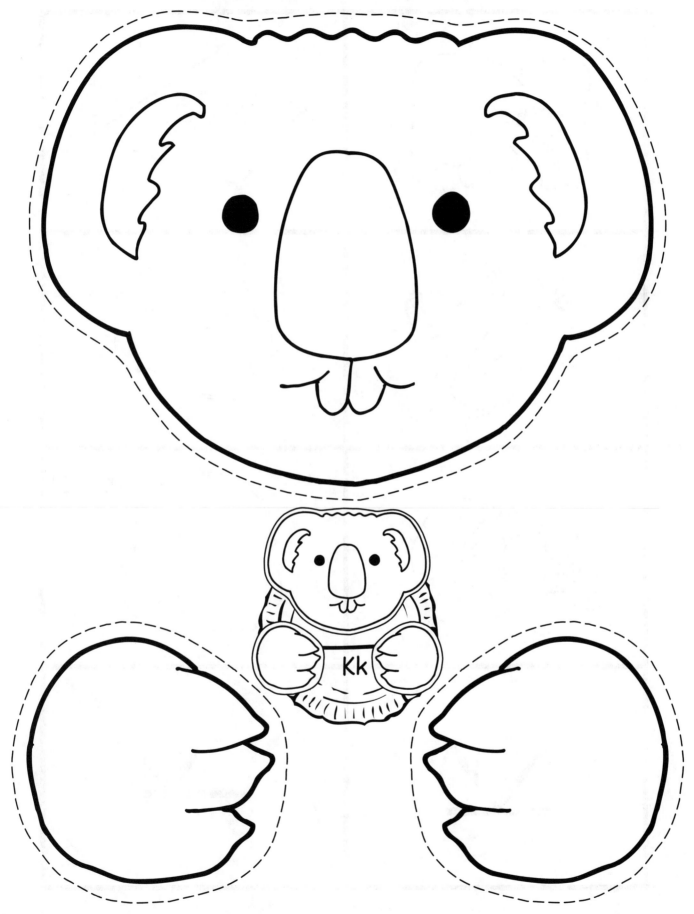

Kk

Letter K Pocket Cards

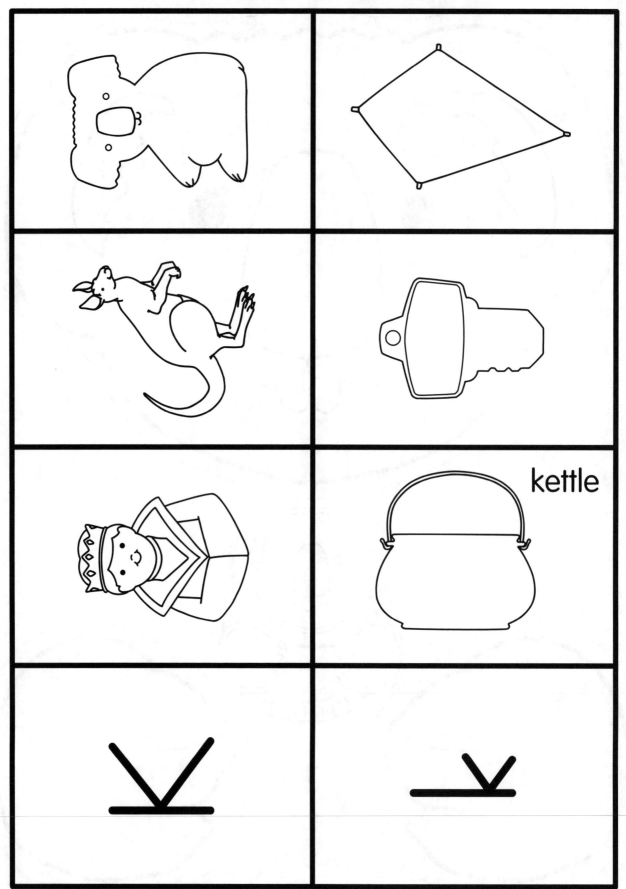

kettle

Lion Pocket Pal

Letter L Pocket Cards

Mouse Pocket Pal

Letter M Pocket Cards

Narwhal Pocket Pal

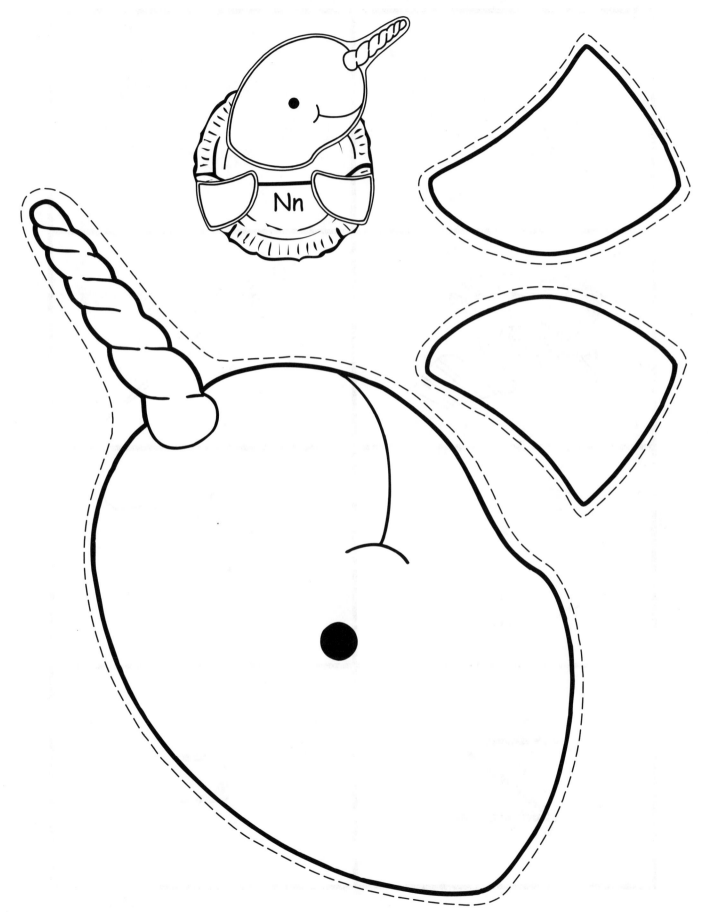

Nn

Letter N Pocket Cards

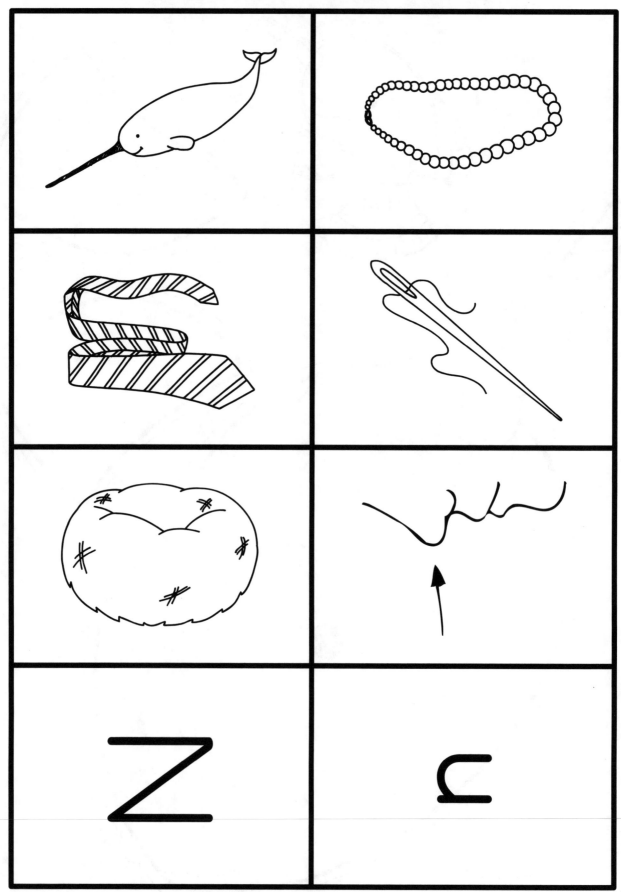

Owl Pocket Pal

Letter O Pocket Cards

Pig Pocket Pal

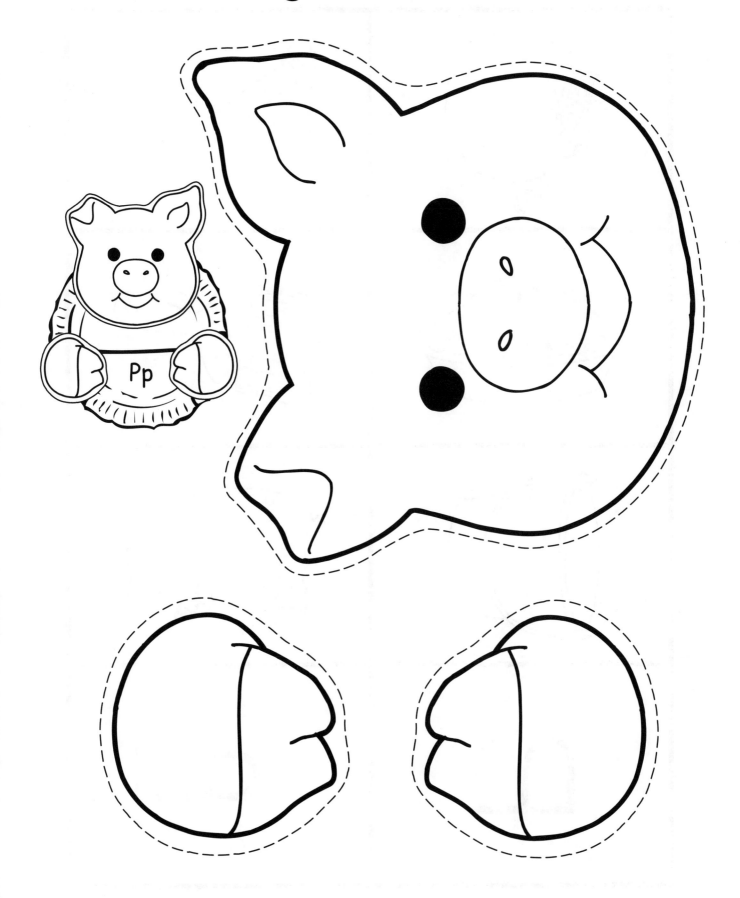

Letter P Pocket Cards

Quail Pocket Pal

Letter Q Pocket Cards

Raccoon Pocket Pal

Letter R Pocket Cards

Seal Pocket Pal

Ss

Letter S Pocket Cards

Tiger Pocket Pal

Letter T Pocket Cards

Unicorn Pocket Pal

Uu

Letter U Pocket Cards

Vulture Pocket Pal

Letter V Pocket Cards

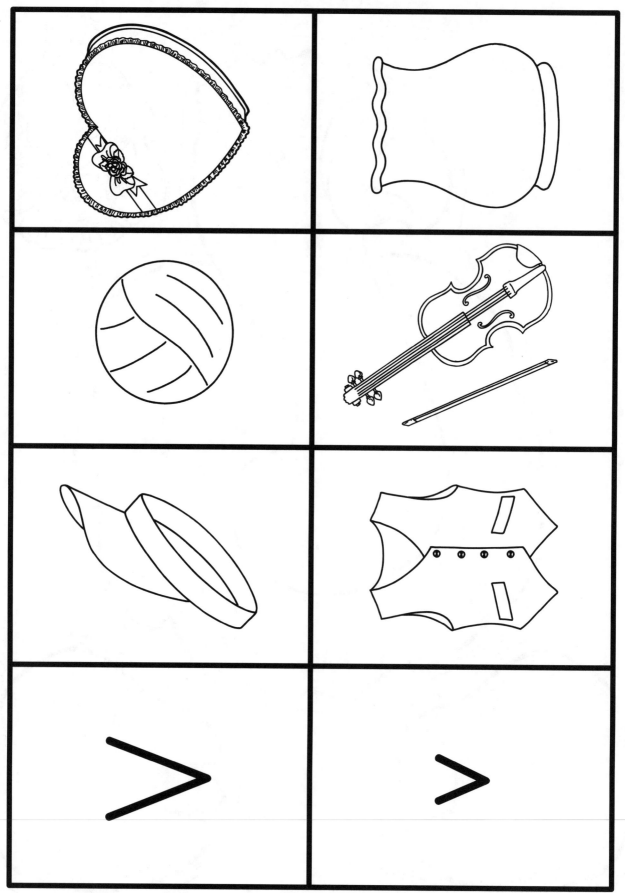

Walrus Pocket Pal

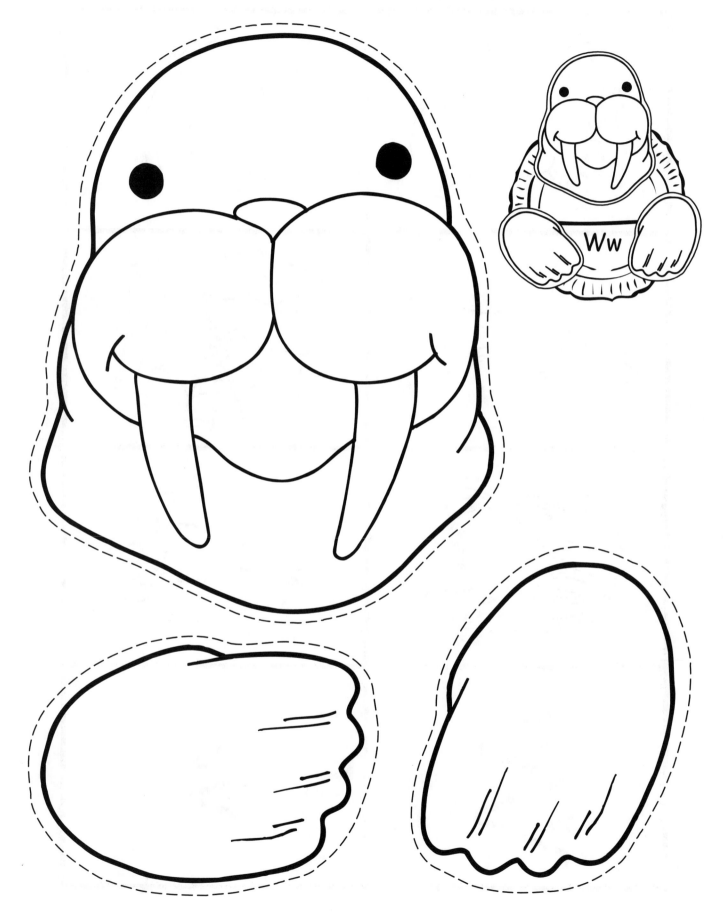

Letter W Pocket Cards

Mister X Pocket Pal

Letter X Pocket Cards

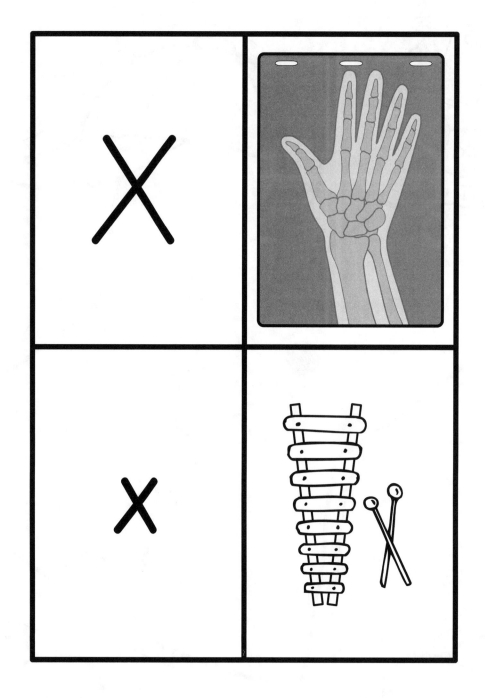

Yak Pocket Pal

Letter Y Pocket Cards

Zebra Pocket Pal

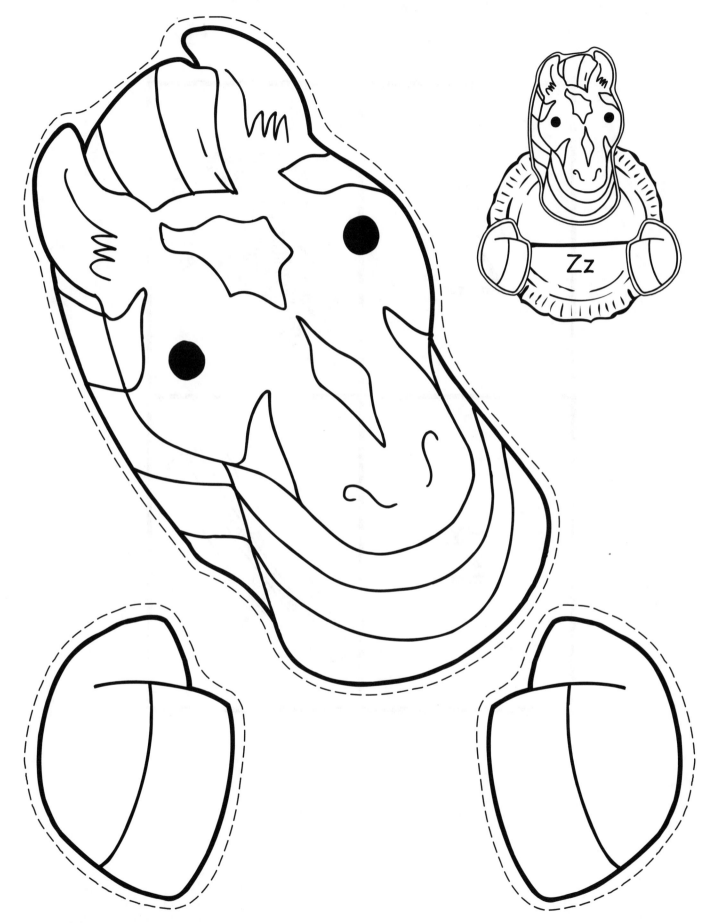

Zz

Letter Z Pocket Cards

Letter Pockets

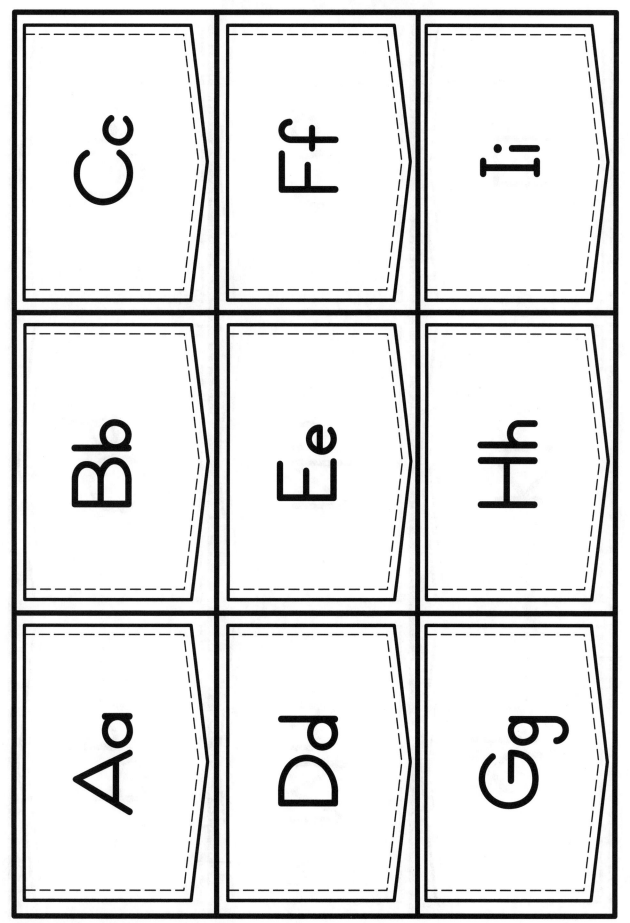

Letter Pockets

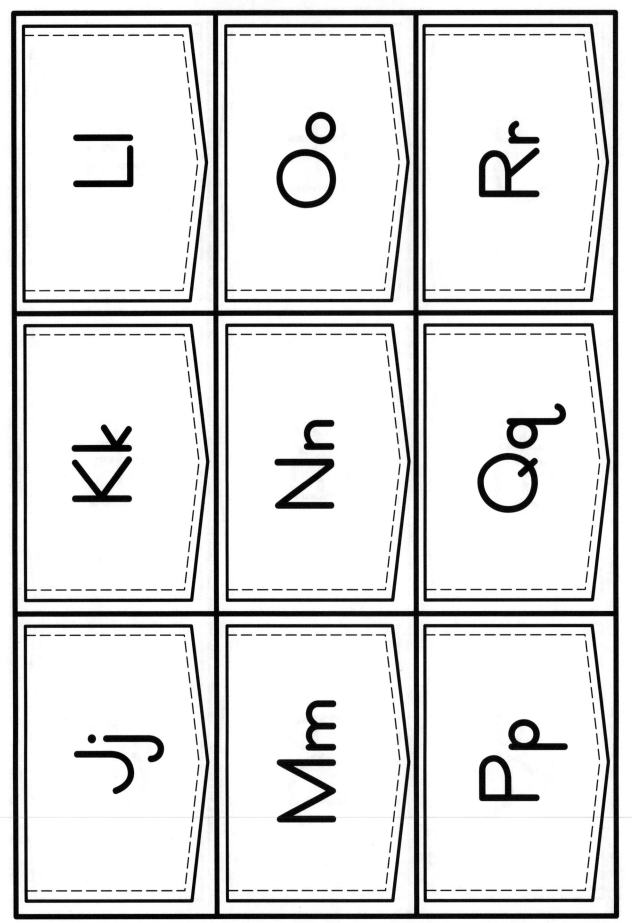

Letter Pockets

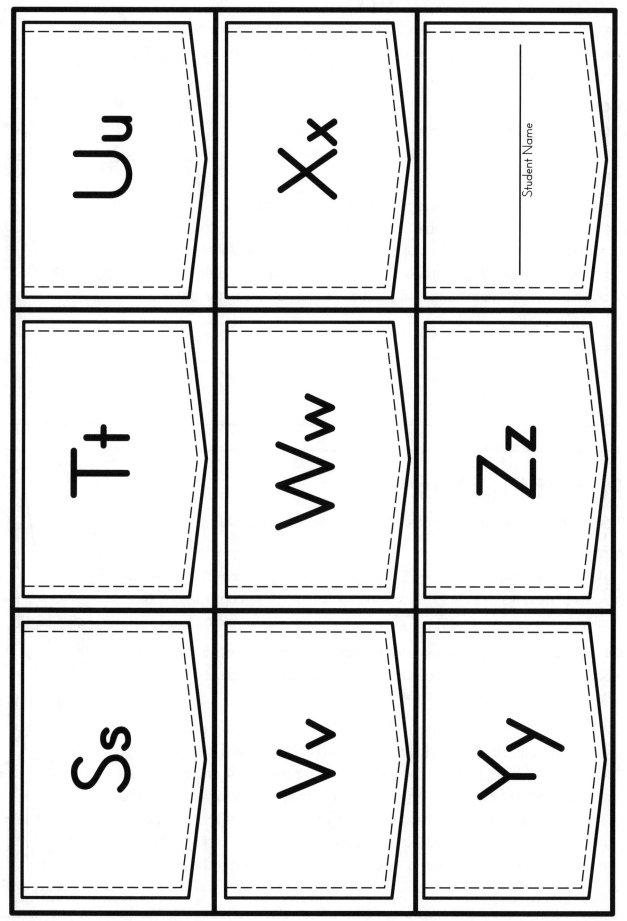

Student Name

Mailbox Pocket Pals

Every child likes to receive mail. Provide materials for children to make personalized Mailbox Pocket Pals to receive notes, awards, birthday cards, and more.

Materials:

Pocket Pals patterns	oak tag	paper plates
crayons or markers	scissors	hole punch
yarn		

Provide each child with an oak tag Pocket Pal to color and cut out. Then help children assemble Pocket Pals (see page 4). Write each child's name on the half pocket. Punch two holes at the top of each child's Pocket Pal. Lace and tie a length of yarn through each hole. Have children hang their Mailbox Pocket Pals along the bottom of a display board.

Pocket Pals Vest

Provide children with brown grocery bags to make alphabet skills practice vests.

Materials:

Pocket Pals patterns	paper plates	brown grocery bags
crayons or markers	scissors	construction paper
stapler	glue	Velcro

Recruit parent volunteers to help children make Pocket Pals vests from brown grocery bags. Each child will need a brown grocery bag and a set of Pocket Pals patterns including matching Pocket Pictures.

Cut a slit along the center of one of the wide panels of a brown grocery bag. Cut two arm holes and a neckline. Reproduce a Pocket Pals pattern and matching Pocket Cards for each child. Then help children assemble (see page 4) and glue Pocket Pals to the backs of their vests. Write the matching upper- and lower-case letters on the front of each vest. Help children attach Velcro squares to the front vest panels and the backs of Pocket Pictures. Have children attach Pocket Pictures to the front of their vests when they are not practicing alphabet matching.

Pocket Pal Mobiles

Decorate your classroom or an alphabet skills practice center with Pocket Pals Mobiles.

Materials:

Pocket Pals patterns	oak tag	paper plates
crayons or markers	scissors	stapler
hole punch	yarn	

Reproduce oak tag Pocket Pals patterns for children to color and cut out. Help children assemble Pocket Pals (see page 4) and cut apart Pocket Pictures. Write the matching upper- and lower-case letters on each half pocket.

Punch a hole at the top of each assembled Pocket Pal. Measure and cut yarn to staple to the top of each matching Pocket Picture then to the Pocket Pal rim. Lace and tie a length of yarn to the top of each Pocket Pal to hang from the ceiling or window frame in your classroom.

Pocket Pal Puppets

Provide children with materials to make alphabet puppets to use as props during an I Know My ABCs sing-a-long.

Materials:

Pocket Pals patterns	oak tag	paper plates
crayons or markers	scissors	stapler
glue	yarn	ribbon
wiggle eyes	pom poms	fabric scraps
Letter Pockets		

Front

Back

Each child will need one and one-half paper plates. Reproduce oak tag Pocket Pals for children to color, cut out, and decorate with a variety of craft supplies (see page 64). Help each child glue the character's head to the back of the whole paper plate. Then glue the matching Letter Pocket below the head and the matching hands, paws, or fins on either side. Write the child's name on the opposite side of the whole plate. Help the child align and staple the -half-plate to the top of the whole plate to form an upside down pocket. Demonstrate how to place your hand inside the pocket to make the puppet move.

Request for Craft Supplies

Dear Parent,

Please send supplies listed below to school with your child for our alphabet practice workstation.

- [ ] yarn
- [ ] ribbon
- [ ] twine
- [ ] shoelaces
- [ ] buttons
- [ ] pom poms
- [ ] pasta noodles (uncooked)
- [ ] paper plates

- [ ] rice (uncooked)
- [ ] glitter
- [ ] glitter pens
- [ ] wiggle eyes
- [ ] sticky dots
- [ ] cotton balls
- [ ] sequins
- [ ] beads

- [ ] cotton swabs
- [ ] craft sticks
- [ ] bottle caps
- [ ] sand
- [ ] seashells
- [ ] pipe cleaners
- [ ] paper clips

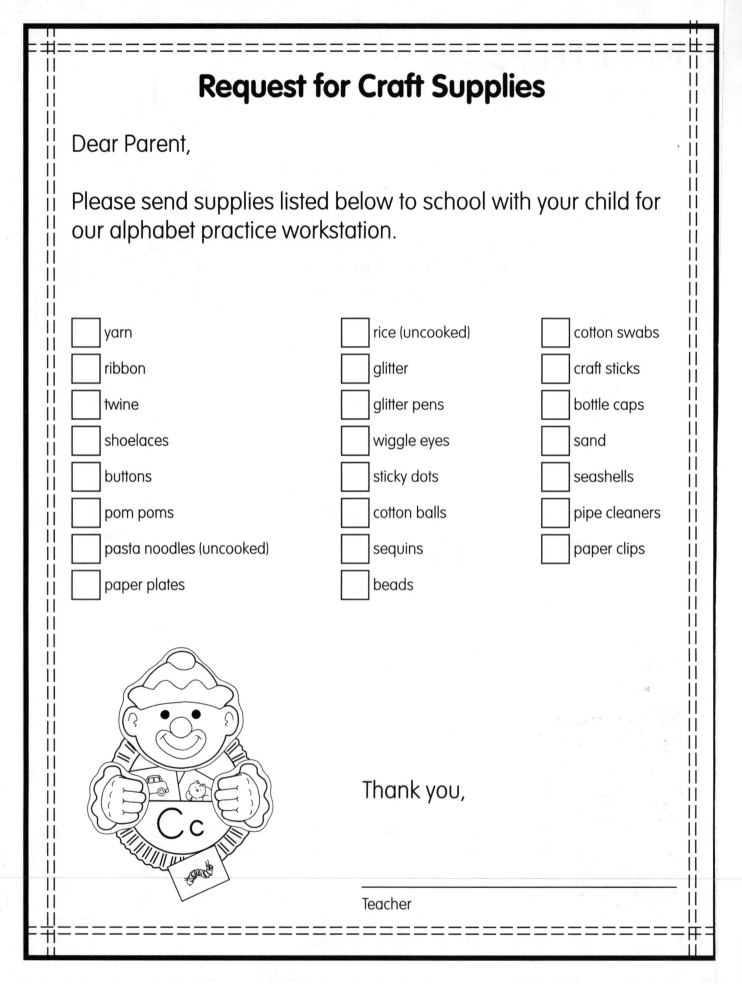

Thank you,

_____

Teacher